# Personal Jurisdiction
# Civil Procedure
# Law Under the Scalpel: Case Dissections
# (Law in Pieces)

Anjanette G. Seymour, LL.M., LL.B. (Hons.)

This work is published as part of the 'Law in Pieces' series study snippets. It is intended as an educational aid and should not be construed as a full textbook or novel. The content herein does not constitute legal advice. Readers should consult authoritative sources and law professors for comprehensive guidance.



Cover Design: Anjanette G. Seymour

ISBN: 9798995892366

## TABLE OF CONTENTS

## Dedication

For every student who has ever felt lost in the maze of jurisdiction. May this book be the light that finally reveals the path.

## Epigraph

*"The law becomes clear the moment we stop memorizing its rules and begin understanding its anatomy."*

**— Anjanette G. Seymour**

## Preface — Law in Pieces

The *Law in Pieces* series was created to transform legal education into something clear, humane, and deeply understandable. Instead of treating doctrine as a list of abstract rules, this series breaks the law into narrative-driven pieces that reveal the logic beneath the surface. Each volume is designed to give students not only knowledge, but epiphany — the moment the law finally makes sense.

*Personal Jurisdiction Civil Procedure Law Under the Scalpel: Case Dissections* is the surgical branch of this mission. Here, cases are dissected with precision, exposing their organs, fractures, and doctrinal lifeblood. The goal is not simplification. It is illumination.

## Preface — Personal Jurisdiction Under the Scalpel: Case Dissections

Personal Jurisdiction can be an intimidating study of the doctrines in Civil Procedure. Students encounter it early; some struggle with it deeply. But the doctrine is not impossible — it is simply layered and evolving.

This volume places Personal Jurisdiction under the scalpel.

Each case is treated as a body on the table. Its heart, spine, brain, lungs, and stomach are examined with care. Its fractures are exposed. Its evolution is traced. Its modern form is revealed. By the end of these dissections, the doctrine becomes not a puzzle, but a living organism with structure, purpose, and logic.

This book helps students see the progression of the cases and understand the doctrine from a clearer, more intuitive point of view. It is for anyone who has ever wondered why Personal Jurisdiction feels harder than it should.

## Author's Note

*Law in Pieces* began with memory.

I earned my first law degree with honours through the University of London's External Programme — a path where I was both the teacher and the student. I taught myself the law. There were no daily lectures, no built-in structure, no professor to reassure me that I belonged. There was only discipline, persistence, and the quiet resolve to keep going even when the material felt distant and unforgiving. Years later, I went on to earn my Master of Laws from an ABA-approved law school. By then, I had crossed jurisdictions, crossed borders, and crossed life stages. I was a mother. I had young children. I had studied law once, long ago, and returned to it again in a new country, under a new system, with new expectations.

I remember struggling in a class and asking a question — only to be told, *"Oh, you're a foreign student. That makes sense that you don't understand this.* "In that moment, the issue was no longer doctrine. It was belonging. That experience stayed with me.

- I know what it feels like to teach yourself law.
- I know what it feels like to move between legal systems.
- I know what it feels like to return to study after years away, carrying responsibility, doubt, and the quiet fear of wondering whether you still belong in the room.

*Law in Pieces* was born from that lived experience. This series is for those who are teaching themselves the law. For those who have studied in one jurisdiction and find themselves learning in another. For those who learn best through narrative, analogy, and connection rather than cold abstraction. For those who have ever felt isolated, incompetent, or tempted to second-guess their journey. These books are not shortcuts. They are bridges. They are designed to make doctrine human — to show how the law fits into real life, real harm, real relationships, and real choices. Each volume breaks complex rules into recognizable patterns, intuitive structures, and stories that stay with you long after the page is turned.

I do not believe the law is meant to be exclusionary. I do not believe confusion is a measure of intelligence. And I do not believe that struggling means you do not belong.

*Law in Pieces* exists to say: **you do belong**. Wherever you are studying from. However you arrived here. Whatever your path has looked like. These books are for you.

Warmly,
Anjanette G. Seymour, LL.M., LL.B. (Hons.)

## Introduction to the Case Dissection Method

**Each case in this volume is dissected using a consistent anatomical framework:**

- The Patient — What the case is and why it matters.
- Presenting Symptoms — Why students struggle with it.
- Facts Under the Scalpel — The essential facts stripped to their functional core.
- Diagnosis — The issue and rule in clean, modern language.
- The Procedure — A step-by-step dissection of the court's reasoning.
- Pathology Report — The holding, rationale, and doctrinal impact.
- Aftercare — How to use the case on exams and in practice.
- Autopsy Notes — Insights, fractures, and epiphanies.

This method is designed to make even the most intimidating cases accessible, memorable, and usable.

# INTRODUCTION

## The Anatomy of Personal Jurisdiction

Personal Jurisdiction is the first great puzzle of Civil Procedure — the doctrine that determines whether a court has the power to touch a defendant at all. It is the circulatory system of litigation, the gateway to every lawsuit, and the source of more 1L confusion than almost any other topic. Students often encounter it as a list of cases, rules, and tests, but beneath that surface lies a living organism with structure, evolution, and purpose.

This book reveals that organism.

Personal Jurisdiction did not emerge fully formed. It grew, fractured, healed, and reshaped itself across more than a century of doctrinal transformation. Each case in its lineage is a body on the table — with a heart, a spine, a brain, lungs, and sometimes fractures that never fully healed. Understanding the doctrine requires understanding those bodies, how they lived, how they died, and how they gave rise to the next.

This volume places each case under the scalpel.

The Evolution of the Doctrine

The story begins with Pennoyer, a rigid territorial skeleton built on sovereignty and physical presence. It was a body too stiff to survive the modern world. International Shoe replaced that skeleton with a beating heart — fairness, minimum contacts, and functional presence. McGee expanded the lungs, allowing a single purposeful contact to sustain jurisdiction. Hanson inserted a spine of purposeful availment, preventing collapse into limitless reach.

Then the doctrine learned to think.

***World-Wide Volkswagen*** distinguished between the foreseeability of product travel and the foreseeability of being sued. ***Burger King*** added muscular structure, showing how contracts create deliberate affiliation.

***Asahi*** fractured the skull, revealing two competing brains in the stream-of-commerce debate — a split that still haunts the doctrine.

Modern cases tightened the bones.

***Goodyear*** and ***Daimler*** shrank general jurisdiction into a narrow, nearly immovable skeleton. ***Bristol-Myers Squibb*** sharpened the scalpel, demanding claim-specific connections. ***Ford Motor Co.*** restored flexibility, clarifying what it means for a claim to "relate to" forum contacts.

Together, these cases form the full anatomical map of Personal Jurisdiction. By the end of this volume, you will not simply know the rules. You will understand the anatomy.

How to Use This Book:

Each case follows a consistent anatomical structure:

- Heart — the core issue
- Spine — the rule of law
- Brain — the reasoning
- Lungs — the tests applied
- Stomach — the facts digested
- Fractures — weaknesses and unresolved tensions
- Future Prognosis — how the case shapes modern doctrine

This method is designed to give you clarity, confidence, and mastery.

The scalpel is in your hand now. Let's begin the dissection.

## Personal Jurisdiction: An Anatomical Introduction

Personal Jurisdiction is the circulatory system of Civil Procedure — the network of connections that determines where a lawsuit may live, breathe, and move. It is the doctrine that decides whether a court has the power to touch a defendant at all. Without it, every case would be a wandering body with no lawful place to rest.

For generations, students have struggled with this doctrine not because it is inherently complex, but because it has evolved through a series of dramatic transformations. Each era reshaped the body: from Pennoyer's rigid territorial skeleton, to International Shoe's living heart, to the modern cases that tighten, refine, and sometimes fracture the doctrine's organs.

This section places the doctrine under the scalpel.

Each case is dissected anatomically — heart, spine, brain, lungs, stomach — so students can see not only what the Court held, but *why* the doctrine changed, *how* it functions, and *where* its weaknesses lie. The goal is not memorization. It is comprehension. It is clarity. It is the moment a student finally sees the living organism beneath the rules.

Across these autopsies, a clear evolution emerges:

- ***Pennoyer*** gives the doctrine its first bones — rigid, territorial, formalistic.
- ***International Shoe*** replaces those bones with a beating heart of fairness and minimum contacts.
- ***McGee*** expands the lungs, allowing a single purposeful contact to sustain jurisdiction.
- ***Hanson*** inserts a spine of purposeful availment, preventing collapse into limitless reach.
- ***World-Wide Volkswagen*** gives the doctrine a reasoning mind, distinguishing product travel from legal foreseeability.

- ***Burger King*** builds muscular structure, showing how contracts create deliberate affiliation.
- ***Asahi*** fractures the skull, revealing two competing brains in the stream-of-commerce debate.
- ***Goodyear*** and ***Daimler*** shrink general jurisdiction into a narrow skeletal frame.
- ***Bristol-Myers Squibb*** sharpens the scalpel, demanding claim-specific connections.
- ***Ford Motor Co.*** restores flexibility, clarifying what it means for a claim to "relate to" forum contacts.

Together, these cases form the full anatomical map of Personal Jurisdiction — its organs, its fractures, its evolution, and its modern shape.

This section is designed to give students: **a coherent, narrative-driven understanding of a doctrine that has confused generations.**

By the end of these dissections, the reader will not simply know the rules. They will understand the body.

# *Pennoyer v. Neff (1877):* Full Legal Autopsy

Civil Procedure's first cadaver is on the table. This is the body that gave the doctrine its original bones — rigid, territorial, formalistic — and whose eventual death made room for the living, breathing organism that became *International Shoe.*

This autopsy follows the full Legal Autopsy method: anatomical, chronological, doctrinal, and unforgettable.

## Identification of the Body

- **Case:** *Pennoyer v. Neff*, 95 U.S. 714 (1877)
- **Doctrine:** Personal Jurisdiction
- **Era:** Post–Civil War formalism
- **Reason for Autopsy:** This case created the original skeleton of jurisdiction — territorial power — and every modern case either fractures, replaces, or refines its bones.

## External Examination

The body presents with:

- A dispute over unpaid legal fees in Oregon
- A default judgment entered without personal service
- A defendant (Neff) who was not physically present in the state
- A lawyer (Mitchell) who sued for fees
- A land seizure that triggered the jurisdictional challenge

The posture is procedural, not substantive: **Was the original judgment valid?**

## Cause of Death

The rigid territorial theory — the idea that a state's power ends at its borders — could not survive:

- Interstate commerce
- Corporate mobility
- National markets
- Long-distance defendants
- Modern transportation and communication

The doctrine died slowly, but *International Shoe* delivered the fatal blow.

**Internal Examination**

**Heart (Core Issue)** Can a state court exercise personal jurisdiction over a nonresident who was not personally served within the state?

**Spine (Rule of Law)** A state has no power over persons or property outside its borders. Jurisdiction requires:

- **In personam:** personal service within the state
- **In rem / quasi in rem:** property attached at the start of the suit

The spine is rigid, inflexible, and formalistic.

**Brain (Reasoning)** The Court reasons from sovereignty, not fairness:

- States are like separate nations
- Power is strictly territorial
- Due process requires physical presence or property seizure

The brain is old-world, pre-modern, and deeply formal.

**Lungs (Tests Applied)** Pennoyer breathes through two categories:

- Presence
- Property

No other oxygen enters the system.

**Stomach (Facts Digested)** The Court focuses on:

- Neff was not in Oregon
- He was not personally served
- His property was seized after judgment

The stomach digests only formal facts, not fairness.

**Toxicology Report**

External forces influencing the decision:

- 19th-century state sovereignty
- Limited travel and communication
- Suspicion of interstate reach
- No national market economy
- No corporate mobility

The doctrine reflects its era's political and social chemistry.

**Fractures and Weak Points**

The body shows multiple fractures:

- Inflexibility
- Formalism
- Artificial categories
- Manipulability (seizing property to create jurisdiction)
- Obsolescence

These fractures made the body unsustainable.

**Surviving Relatives**

Even after death, Pennoyer left behind organs that still function:

- Service of process rules
- In rem jurisdiction
- Due process limits on state power
- The requirement of notice

These bones remain in the modern body.

**Future Prognosis**

Pennoyer's doctrine is dead, but its DNA lives on in:

- Purposeful availment
- Fairness and reasonableness
- The need for a connection between defendant and forum
- Constitutional limits on state power

Modern cases like *Daimler* and *Bristol-Myers* echo Pennoyer's territorial instincts — old bones sometimes reappear.

**Variable Manipulation**

Changing one fact alters the outcome dramatically:

- Personal service in Oregon → jurisdiction valid
- Property seized before judgment → quasi in rem jurisdiction valid
- Contract formed while Neff was physically in Oregon → purposeful presence

This teaches students how jurisdiction turns on tiny factual shifts.

**Mini Lab:**

Suppose Neff owned a small cabin in Oregon at the time Mitchell sued him, but Mitchell did not seize it until after judgment. Does the court have jurisdiction under *Pennoyer*? Why or why no?

## *International Shoe Co. v. Washington (1945):* Full Legal Autopsy

International Shoe is the moment the doctrine receives a new heart. Pennoyer's rigid skeleton is still on the table, but now the body begins to breathe—flexible, functional, and capable of living in a modern world. This is the case that transforms a confused student into someone who finally *understands* personal jurisdiction.

### Identification of the Body

- **Case:** *International Shoe Co. v. Washington*, 326 U.S. 310 (1945)
- **Doctrine:** Personal Jurisdiction
- **Era:** Rise of national commerce and corporate mobility
- **Reason for Autopsy:** This case replaces Pennoyer's rigid bones with a living, breathing standard: **minimum contacts**.

### External Examination

The body presents with:

- A Delaware corporation headquartered in Missouri
- Salesmen living and working in Washington
- No physical office, warehouse, or formal presence in the state
- A dispute over unpaid unemployment taxes
- A central question: **Can Washington assert jurisdiction over a corporation that is not "present" in the Pennoyer sense?**

This is the moment the old skeleton cracks.

### Internal Examination

**Heart (Core Issue)** Can a state exercise jurisdiction over an out-of-state corporation based on its activities within the state, even if the corporation is not physically present?

**Spine (Rule of Law)** Jurisdiction is proper when the defendant has **minimum contacts** with the forum such that the suit does not offend **traditional notions of fair play and substantial justice**. This becomes the new backbone of the doctrine.

**Brain (Reasoning)** The Court reasons from fairness, not sovereignty:

- Presence is functional, not physical
- A corporation acts through its agents
- Continuous and systematic activities justify jurisdiction
- Occasional or isolated contacts may not

The brain shifts from rigid territorial logic to practical reality.

**Lungs (Tests Applied)** The doctrine now breathes through:

- Continuous and systematic contacts
- Single or occasional acts
- Quality and nature of contacts
- Relationship between contacts and the claim

This is the oxygen Pennoyer never had.

**Stomach (Facts Digested)** The Court digests:

- Salesmen residing in Washington
- Regular solicitation of business
- Orders sent to Missouri but fulfilled nationwide
- Benefits and protections received from Washington law

These facts are metabolized into the new minimum contacts test.

**Cause of Death (for Pennoyer)**

Pennoyer's territorial rigidity could not survive:

- Corporate mobility
- Interstate commerce
- National markets
- Modern transportation
- Fairness-based reasoning

International Shoe performs the autopsy that ends Pennoyer's dominance.

### Toxicology Report

External forces shaping the decision:

- Post-Depression economic restructuring
- Rise of national corporations
- Increased interstate travel
- States' need to regulate out-of-state businesses
- A more realistic understanding of corporate presence

The doctrine reflects a modernizing America.

### Fractures and Weak Points

Even this new body has fractures:

- "Minimum contacts" is inherently vague
- Fairness is subjective
- Courts disagree on what counts as "systematic"
- The test invites balancing, not bright lines

These fractures later split open in *Asahi* and tighten in *Daimler.*

### Surviving Relatives

International Shoe gives birth to:

- **Purposeful availment** (*Hanson*)
- **Foreseeability limits** (*World-Wide Volkswagen*)
- **Contractual contacts** (*Burger King*)
- **Stream of commerce debates** (*Asahi*)
- **"At home" general jurisdiction** (*Goodyear*, *Daimler*)

Every modern case is a descendant.

**Future Prognosis**

International Shoe remains the beating heart of personal jurisdiction. Even as:

- general jurisdiction shrinks, and
- specific jurisdiction tightens,

the doctrine still pulses with:

- fairness
- reasonableness
- purposeful connection

It is the living core of the modern body.

**Variable Manipulation**

Changing one fact changes the outcome:

- Salesmen as independent contractors → weaker contacts
- A warehouse in Washington → strong general jurisdiction
- A claim unrelated to Washington activities → specific jurisdiction fails

This teaches students how to think like lawyers.

**Mini Lab:**

Suppose International Shoe's salesmen only visited Washington twice a year for trade shows, with no regular solicitation. Would Washington have jurisdiction under the minimum contacts test?

## *McGee v. International Life Insurance Co. (1957)*: Full Legal Autopsy

This is the next body on the table because it shows the doctrine taking its first breath after *International Shoe*. Shoe gave the doctrine a heart; **McGee fills its lungs with air**. It is short, deceptively simple, and absolutely essential for students who struggle with personal jurisdiction.

### Identification of the Body

- **Case:** *McGee v. International Life Insurance Co.*, 355 U.S. 220 (1957)
- **Doctrine:** Personal Jurisdiction
- **Era:** Post-Shoe expansion
- **Reason for Autopsy:** This case proves that **one single, purposeful contact** can be enough for jurisdiction when the state has a strong interest.

### External Examination

The body presents with:

- A California resident holding a life insurance policy
- A Texas insurance company with **no offices, agents, or property** in California
- A single policy mailed into the state
- A refusal to pay the beneficiary
- A central question: **Is one contact enough?**

This is the first real test of Shoe's new heart.

### Internal Examination

**Heart (Core Issue)** Can a state assert jurisdiction over a nonresident corporation based on **one deliberate, purposeful contact**?

**Spine (Rule of Law)** A single, intentional contact can satisfy minimum contacts when:

- The contact is purposeful
- The claim arises directly from that contact
- The state has a strong regulatory interest

This becomes the doctrine's new backbone.

**Brain (Reasoning)** The Court reasons from fairness and state interest:

- The insurer **solicited** the policy
- The contract was delivered in California
- Premiums were mailed from California
- California had a strong interest in protecting its residents

The brain is now fully functional—flexible, realistic, and fairness-driven.

**Lungs (Tests Applied)** McGee expands the doctrine's breathing capacity through:

- The **single contact rule**
- State interest analysis
- Purposeful solicitation
- Direct connection between contact and claim

This is the oxygen that allows the doctrine to grow.

**Stomach (Facts Digested)** The Court digests:

- The insurer reached into California
- The contract was formed there

- The insured lived and died there
- The dispute arose from that single contact

These facts are enough to sustain jurisdiction.

**Cause of Death (for Pennoyer's Remnants)**

McGee kills the idea that jurisdiction requires:

- Physical presence
- Multiple contacts
- Continuous activity

The old bones crack further.

**Toxicology Report**

External forces influencing the decision:

- Growth of national insurance markets
- Consumer protection concerns
- Increased interstate communication
- States' interest in regulating out-of-state companies

The doctrine reflects a modern, interconnected economy.

**Fractures and Weak Points**

Even this expanded body has fractures:

- How far can "single contact" go?
- What counts as purposeful solicitation?
- Does state interest always matter?
- How does this fit with *Hanson*'s later limits?

These fractures will be exposed in the next autopsy.

### Surviving Relatives

McGee gives birth to:

- The principle that **quality > quantity** of contacts
- The importance of state interest
- The requirement that claims arise from the contact

These organs remain alive in modern specific jurisdiction.

### Future Prognosis

McGee remains a strong example of:

- Purposeful availment
- Direct connection
- Fairness
- State interest

But its broad reach is later restrained by *Hanson v. Denckla*, which adds a spine of limitation.

### Variable Manipulation

Changing one fact changes the outcome:

- If the insurer had **not** solicited the policy → weaker contact
- If the claim did **not** arise from the policy → no specific jurisdiction
- If the insured moved to California **after** buying the policy → weaker state interest

This teaches students how to analyze fact patterns.

### Mini Lab:

Suppose the insurer mailed a single advertisement to California residents, but the insured purchased the policy while visiting Texas. Does California have jurisdiction under *McGee*?

## *Hanson v. Denckla (1958):* Full Legal Autopsy

Hanson is the moment the doctrine stiffens. After McGee's generous breath of expansion, Hanson inserts a backbone — a requirement that the defendant must **purposefully avail** itself of the forum. Without this spine, the doctrine would collapse under the weight of limitless jurisdiction. This autopsy shows students exactly why Hanson matters and how it shapes every modern case.

### Identification of the Body

- **Case:** *Hanson v. Denckla*, 357 U.S. 235 (1958)
- **Doctrine:** Personal Jurisdiction
- **Era:** Post-McGee contraction
- **Reason for Autopsy:** It introduces **purposeful availment**, the backbone of modern specific jurisdiction.

### External Examination

The body presents with:

- A trust created in Delaware
- A settlor who later moved to Florida
- A dispute over the trust's validity
- A Florida court attempting to assert jurisdiction over a Delaware trustee
- A central question: **Did the trustee create contacts with Florida, or did the settlor create them unilaterally?**

This is the first real test of McGee's expansion.

### Internal Examination

**Heart (Core Issue)** Can a state assert jurisdiction over a defendant when all the defendant's contacts with the forum arise from the **unilateral actions** of someone else?

**Spine (Rule of Law)** The defendant must **purposefully avail** itself of the privilege of conducting activities within the forum state. This becomes the doctrine's backbone — the structural support that prevents overreach.

**Brain (Reasoning)** The Court reasons from defendant-centered fairness:

- The trustee did not reach into Florida
- The settlor moved there on her own
- The trustee did not solicit Florida business
- The trustee's only connection to Florida was the settlor's relocation

The brain shifts from McGee's state-interest focus to a defendant-focused analysis.

**Lungs (Tests Applied)** Hanson tightens the breathing room:

- Contacts must be purposeful, not accidental
- Contacts must be created by the defendant, not the plaintiff
- Contacts must show deliberate affiliation with the forum

This is the oxygen that keeps the doctrine balanced.

**Stomach (Facts Digested)** The Court digests:

- The trust was created in Delaware
- Administered in Delaware
- Governed by Delaware law
- The trustee never solicited Florida business
- The settlor's move was unilateral

These facts do not satisfy purposeful availment.

**Cause of Death (for McGee's Broad Reach)**

Hanson kills the idea that:

- A single contact is always enough
- State interest alone can justify jurisdiction
- Plaintiff-created contacts count

The doctrine becomes more disciplined.

**Toxicology Report**

External forces influencing the decision:

- Concern about states overreaching
- Desire to protect out-of-state defendants
- Post-war economic caution
- Fear of unlimited jurisdiction

The doctrine reflects a need for structural restraint.

**Fractures and Weak Points**

Even this backbone has fractures:

- What counts as "purposeful"?
- How much activity is enough?
- Do digital contacts count?
- How does modern mobility complicate the analysis?

These fractures later split open in *World-Wide Volkswagen* and *Asahi.*

**Surviving Relatives**

Hanson gives birth to:

- The purposeful availment requirement
- The rule that unilateral acts don't count
- The idea that defendant-created contacts are essential

These organs remain vital in every modern case.

**Future Prognosis**

Hanson remains the spine of personal jurisdiction:

- It limits McGee
- It shapes *World-Wide Volkswagen*
- It anchors *Burger King*
- It complicates *Asahi*
- It underlies *Bristol-Myers*

Without Hanson, the doctrine would collapse.

**Variable Manipulation**

Changing one fact changes the outcome:

- If the trustee had solicited Florida business → purposeful availment
- If the trust had been administered partly in Florida → stronger contacts
- If the trustee had mailed documents into Florida → closer to McGee

This teaches students how to analyze fact patterns with precision.

**Mini Lab:**

Suppose the trustee sent annual statements and account updates to the settlor after she moved to Florida. Does this create purposeful availment under *Hanson*?

## *World-Wide Volkswagen Corp. v. Woodson (1980):* Full Legal Autopsy

This is the cadaver that teaches the doctrine how to reason. It clarifies that **foreseeability of product travel is not the same as foreseeability of being sued**, and it tightens the doctrine after McGee's expansion and Hanson's backbone. This autopsy shows students exactly why World-Wide Volkswagen matters and how it shapes every modern case.

### Identification of the Body

- **Case:** *World-Wide Volkswagen Corp. v. Woodson*, 444 U.S. 286 (1980)
- **Doctrine:** Personal Jurisdiction
- **Era:** Post-Hanson tightening
- **Reason for Autopsy:** It draws the line between predictable movement and purposeful targeting, giving the doctrine a **thinking mind**.

### External Examination

The body presents with:

- A New York family driving to Arizona
- A car accident in Oklahoma
- A regional dealer and distributor operating **only in New York**
- No advertising, offices, or sales in Oklahoma
- A central question: **Is it enough that a product might foreseeably end up in another state?**

This is where the doctrine confronts the limits of fairness.

### Internal Examination

**Heart (Core Issue)** Does a defendant's product ending up in a forum state — through the unilateral actions of a consumer — create personal jurisdiction?

**Spine (Rule of Law)** The defendant must **purposefully avail** itself of the forum; mere foreseeability that a product might travel there is not enough. This spine builds directly on *Hanson.*

**Brain (Reasoning)** This is the case where the doctrine develops a brain — the ability to distinguish between two types of foreseeability:

- **Foreseeability of product travel** → not enough
- **Foreseeability of being haled into court** → requires purposeful targeting

The Court reasons:

- The dealer did not advertise in Oklahoma
- Did not sell cars there
- Did not deliver cars there
- Did not cultivate the Oklahoma market
- The only connection was the consumer's unilateral decision to drive through the state

The brain is now fully formed: defendant-centered, purposeful, and logical.

**Lungs (Tests Applied)** The doctrine breathes through:

- Purposeful availment
- Defendant-created contacts
- Reasonable anticipation of suit
- Fairness and foreseeability

These tests oxygenate the modern doctrine.

**Stomach (Facts Digested)** The Court digests:

- The dealer's business was strictly local
- No intentional reach into Oklahoma
- No stream-of-commerce distribution
- No purposeful affiliation

These facts do not satisfy minimum contacts.

**Cause of Death (for Broad Foreseeability)**

This case kills the idea that:

- A product's mobility creates jurisdiction
- Consumer travel creates jurisdiction
- Foreseeability alone is enough

The doctrine becomes more disciplined and defendant-focused.

**Toxicology Report**

External forces influencing the decision:

- Fear of unlimited jurisdiction
- Concern about burdening small businesses
- Desire to protect defendants from nationwide exposure
- Post-1970s economic caution

The doctrine reflects a need for predictable limits.

**Fractures and Weak Points**

Even this brain has fractures:

- What counts as "purposeful"?
- How much targeting is enough?

- What about national brands?
- What about modern e-commerce?

These fractures will later split open in *Asahi*.

**Surviving Relatives**

World-Wide Volkswagen strengthens:

- Hanson's purposeful availment
- Shoe's fairness
- McGee's connection requirement

It becomes the intellectual core of modern specific jurisdiction.

**Future Prognosis**

This case remains essential because it:

- Limits jurisdiction
- Protects defendants
- Clarifies foreseeability
- Shapes modern analysis in *Bristol-Myers* and *Ford Motor Co.*

It is the doctrine's reasoning center.

**Variable Manipulation**

Changing one fact changes the outcome:

- If the dealer advertised in Oklahoma → purposeful availment
- If the dealer sold cars near the border → stronger contacts
- If the dealer shipped cars into Oklahoma → stream of commerce

This teaches students how to analyze foreseeability correctly.

**Mini Lab:**

Suppose the dealer regularly sold cars to customers who lived near the Oklahoma border and knew many would drive into Oklahoma. Does this create purposeful availment under *World-Wide Volkswagen*?

## *Burger King Corp. v. Rudzewicz (1985):* Full Legal Autopsy

This cadaver is muscular, layered, and multi-factor. It teaches students how purposeful availment works in the context of contracts, and why fairness is not a soft idea — it is a structured, analyzable organ. This is the case that gives the doctrine strength, nuance, and the ability to flex.

### Identification of the Body

- **Case:** *Burger King Corp. v. Rudzewicz*, 471 U.S. 462 (1985)
- **Doctrine:** Personal Jurisdiction
- **Era:** Post-Volkswagen refinement
- **Reason for Autopsy:** It shows that contracts can create purposeful availment, and that jurisdiction is a **multi-factor, muscular analysis** — not a single test.

### External Examination

The body presents with:

- A Michigan franchisee
- A Florida franchisor (Burger King headquarters)
- A long-term franchise relationship
- Negotiations, training, payments, and supervision
- A central question: **Does a contract with an out-of-state company create jurisdiction?**

This is where the doctrine gains strength.

### Internal Examination

**Heart (Core Issue)** Does entering into a long-term, structured contractual relationship with a forum resident create purposeful availment, even without physical presence?

**Spine (Rule of Law)** A contract alone does not automatically establish jurisdiction, but:

- Negotiations
- Course of dealing
- Ongoing obligations
- Deliberate affiliation

can create purposeful availment. This spine is flexible but strong.

**Brain (Reasoning)** The Court reasons through relationship-based foreseeability:

- The franchisee reached out to Florida
- Negotiated with Florida headquarters
- Entered a 20-year relationship governed by Florida law
- Made payments to Florida
- Received supervision and training from Florida

The brain concludes: **This is not random or accidental — it is deliberate.**

**Muscles (Multi-Factor Test)** This is where the doctrine flexes. The Court examines:

- Prior negotiations
- Future consequences
- Terms of the contract
- Actual course of dealing
- Choice-of-law clause
- Length and depth of the relationship

These muscles give the doctrine strength and nuance.

**Lungs (Fairness Factors)** The doctrine breathes through:

- Burden on the defendant
- Forum state's interest
- Plaintiff's interest in convenient relief
- Interstate judicial efficiency
- Shared social policies

Fairness is not vague — it is structured oxygen.

**Stomach (Facts Digested)** The Court digests:

- A 20-year franchise agreement
- Continuous payments to Florida
- Regular communication with Florida
- Training and supervision from Florida
- A deliberate, ongoing relationship

These facts show purposeful availment.

**Cause of Death (for simplistic "no physical presence" arguments)**

Burger King kills the idea that:

- Physical presence is required
- Contracts are irrelevant
- Fairness is unstructured
- Purposeful availment is only about geography

The doctrine becomes muscular and relational.

**Toxicology Report**

External forces influencing the decision:

- Rise of national franchises
- Growth of long-distance business relationships
- Need for predictable rules for interstate commerce
- Increasing complexity of corporate structures

The doctrine reflects a modern, interconnected economy.

## Fractures and Weak Points

Even this muscular body has fractures:

- How much negotiation is enough?
- Do choice-of-law clauses matter too much?
- What about small businesses vs. large corporations?
- How do courts weigh fairness factors?

These fractures will later appear in *Asahi* and *Ford Motor Co.*

## Surviving Relatives

Burger King strengthens:

- Hanson's purposeful availment
- Shoe's fairness
- Volkswagen's foreseeability
- McGee's connection requirement

It becomes the doctrine's muscular core.

## Future Prognosis

This case remains essential because it:

- Defines contractual purposeful availment
- Shapes modern e-commerce jurisdiction

- Influences digital-contact cases
- Guides courts in multi-factor balancing

It is the doctrine's strength and structure.

**Variable Manipulation**

Changing one fact changes the outcome:

- If the franchisee had never negotiated with Florida → weaker contacts
- If payments were made only to Michigan → weaker affiliation
- If the contract had no Florida choice-of-law clause → less foreseeability

This teaches students how to analyze contracts in jurisdiction.

**Mini Lab:**

Suppose the franchisee signed a standard contract with no negotiation, and all communication was with a regional office in Illinois, not Florida. Does Florida still have jurisdiction under *Burger King*?

## *Asahi Metal Industry Co. v. Superior Court (1987):* Full Legal Autopsy

This is the cadaver with the fractured skull — two competing brains inside one head. It is the case that exposes the deepest fault line in personal jurisdiction: **What counts as "purposeful availment" in the stream of commerce?** No majority opinion resolves the split, leaving the doctrine with two incompatible nervous systems.

### Identification of the Body

- **Case:** *Asahi Metal Industry Co. v. Superior Court*, 480 U.S. 102 (1987)
- **Doctrine:** Personal Jurisdiction — Stream of Commerce
- **Era:** Post-Burger King fragmentation
- **Reason for Autopsy:** It creates two competing tests for stream-of-commerce cases, and no majority resolves the split.

### External Examination

The body presents with:

- A motorcycle accident in California
- A Taiwanese tire-tube manufacturer (Cheng Shin)
- A Japanese valve-stem manufacturer (Asahi)
- A third-party indemnity claim
- A central question: **Does placing a component into the stream of commerce create jurisdiction where the final product ends up?**

This is where the doctrine fractures.

### Internal Examination

**Heart (Core Issue)** Does a foreign component manufacturer purposefully avail itself of a forum when its product ends up there through the stream of commerce?

**Spine (Rule of Law)** There is no single rule — instead, two competing spines:

- **O'Connor's Stream of Commerce PLUS**
- **Brennan's Pure Stream of Commerce**

The body has two backbones, and they do not align.

**The Two Brains (Competing Reasoning)**

**Brain A — Justice O'Connor (Plurality)**

**Stream of Commerce PLUS** Placing a product into the stream of commerce is not enough. The defendant must do something more to target the forum.

Examples of "PLUS":

- Advertising in the forum
- Designing the product for the forum
- Establishing channels for customer service
- Marketing through a distributor targeting the forum

Under this brain, Asahi did **not** purposefully avail.

**Brain B — Justice Brennan (Concurrence)**

**Pure Stream of Commerce** If the defendant knows its product is being sold in the forum, that is enough.

Key principles:

- Awareness = purposeful availment
- No "plus" required
- Volume and regularity matter

Under this brain, Asahi likely **did** purposefully avail.

**Why students struggle**

They are taught "stream of commerce," but not that the doctrine has **two incompatible brains**. Your autopsy makes this visible.

**Lungs (Fairness Factors)**

All Justices agree on one thing: **Even if minimum contacts exist, jurisdiction is NOT fair.**

Fairness factors:

- Severe burden on a foreign defendant
- Minimal interest of California (only indemnity claim remained)
- Weak connection to the forum
- International comity concerns

The lungs collapse — fairness suffocates jurisdiction.

**Stomach (Facts Digested)**

The Court digests:

- Asahi sold valve stems to Cheng Shin in Taiwan
- Cheng Shin sold finished tires worldwide
- Asahi did not advertise, sell, or target California
- Only a third-party indemnity claim remained
- California's interest was minimal

These facts do not support jurisdiction under any fairness analysis.

**Cause of Death**

Asahi kills the idea that:

- Stream of commerce is simple
- Awareness alone is always enough
- Fairness is secondary
- International defendants can be haled into U.S. courts easily

The doctrine becomes fractured and uncertain.

**Toxicology Report**

External forces influencing the decision:

- Globalization of manufacturing
- Rise of international supply chains
- Concern about burdening foreign defendants
- Diplomatic and trade considerations
- Fear of unpredictable jurisdictional exposure

The doctrine reflects a world becoming economically interconnected.

**Fractures and Weak Points**

This skull is cracked in multiple places:

- No majority rule
- Two competing tests
- Courts split for decades
- No clear guidance for component manufacturers
- Fairness analysis overshadows contacts

These fractures remain unresolved until *Ford Motor Co. v. Montana* (2021), which softens but does not eliminate the split.

**Surviving Relatives**

Asahi influences:

- *J. McIntyre v. Nicastro* (2011) — still fractured
- *Ford Motor Co.* (2021) — clarifies "relates to" but not stream of commerce
- Modern e-commerce cases
- Global supply chain jurisdiction

It remains a ghost haunting the doctrine.

**Future Prognosis**

Asahi's split persists:

- Some courts follow O'Connor (PLUS)
- Some follow Brennan (pure stream)
- Some blend both
- Some avoid the issue entirely and decide on fairness

The doctrine remains fractured, but your autopsy gives students a map.

**Variable Manipulation**

Changing one fact changes the outcome:

- If Asahi advertised in California → purposeful availment under PLUS
- If Asahi designed valve stems specifically for California motorcycles → PLUS satisfied
- If Asahi had a U.S. distributor targeting California → purposeful availment under both tests

This teaches students how to analyze stream-of-commerce fact patterns.

**Mini Lab:**

Suppose Asahi placed warning labels in English on its valve stems because it knew many would be sold in the United States. Does this satisfy "stream of commerce PLUS"?

## *Goodyear Dunlop Tires Operations, S.A. v. Brown (2011):* Full Legal Autopsy

This is the cadaver that shrinks general jurisdiction from a broad, flexible idea into a narrow, almost skeletal doctrine. It introduces the "at home" standard and signals the death of expansive general jurisdiction. Daimler will later tighten these bones even further, but Goodyear is where the contraction begins.

### Identification of the Body

- **Case:** *Goodyear Dunlop Tires Operations, S.A. v. Brown*, 564 U.S. 915 (2011)
- **Doctrine:** General Personal Jurisdiction
- **Era:** Modern contraction
- **Reason for Autopsy:** It introduces the **"at home"** standard and signals the end of broad general jurisdiction.

### External Examination

The body presents with:

- A bus accident in France
- Foreign subsidiaries of Goodyear (Turkey, France, Luxembourg)
- A lawsuit filed in North Carolina
- Only a small number of tires reaching NC through the stream of commerce
- A central question: **Can a corporation be sued for anything, anywhere it sells products?**

This is where the doctrine begins to tighten.

### Internal Examination

**Heart (Core Issue)** When can a court exercise general jurisdiction over a corporation for claims **unrelated** to the forum?

**Spine (Rule of Law)** A corporation is subject to general jurisdiction only where it is **"at home."** This usually means:

- Place of incorporation
- Principal place of business

This spine is rigid and narrow.

**Brain (Reasoning)** The Court reasons from predictability and fairness:

- General jurisdiction cannot be based on random or limited sales
- The foreign subsidiaries did not target North Carolina
- Their connection to the state was "attenuated" and "sporadic"
- Allowing general jurisdiction here would make corporations suable everywhere

The brain is now focused on limiting exposure.

**Bones (General Jurisdiction Structure)** Goodyear defines the bones of general jurisdiction:

- It is **exceptional**, not routine
- It requires **continuous and systematic** contacts
- But even continuous sales are not enough
- The corporation must be **essentially at home**

These bones will harden further in *Daimler*.

**Lungs (Tests Applied)** The doctrine breathes through:

- Predictability
- Corporate identity

- Fairness to defendants
- Avoiding universal jurisdiction

The lungs are tight and controlled.

**Stomach (Facts Digested)** The Court digests:

- The subsidiaries were foreign companies
- They had no offices in NC
- No employees in NC
- No bank accounts in NC
- Only a small number of tires reached NC through distributors

These facts do not support general jurisdiction.

**Cause of Death**

Goodyear kills the idea that:

- "Continuous and systematic" sales alone create general jurisdiction
- Corporations can be sued anywhere they sell products
- Stream of commerce can support general jurisdiction

The doctrine becomes skeletal and narrow.

**Toxicology Report**

External forces influencing the decision:

- Globalization of corporations
- Concern about forum shopping
- Desire for predictable jurisdictional rules
- International comity

- Fear of exposing corporations to worldwide litigation

The doctrine reflects a need for restraint.

### Fractures and Weak Points

Even this tightened skeleton has fractures:

- What does "at home" really mean?
- Are there exceptions?
- How do courts treat large multinational corporations?
- What about temporary headquarters or major operations?

These fractures will be addressed — and tightened — in *Daimler*.

### Surviving Relatives

Goodyear strengthens:

- Shoe's fairness
- Hanson's purposeful availment (for specific jurisdiction)
- Volkswagen's foreseeability limits
- Asahi's caution about international defendants

It becomes the foundation for modern general jurisdiction.

### Future Prognosis

Goodyear remains essential because it:

- Introduces the "at home" test
- Limits general jurisdiction to rare cases
- Sets the stage for *Daimler*, which will make the doctrine even narrower
- Influences modern cases involving multinational corporations

It is the doctrine's skeletal frame.

**Variable Manipulation**

Changing one fact changes the outcome:

- If the subsidiaries had a warehouse in NC → stronger contacts
- If they were incorporated in NC → general jurisdiction
- If NC was their principal place of business → general jurisdiction

This teaches students how to analyze corporate identity.

**Mini Lab:**

Suppose the foreign subsidiaries sold 10% of their total tire output directly to North Carolina distributors every year. Would that make them "at home" under *Goodyear.*

## *Daimler AG v. Bauman (2014):* Full Legal Autopsy

This is the cadaver that kills broad general jurisdiction. It transforms the doctrine from a flexible idea into a nearly immovable skeleton. After Goodyear narrowed the doctrine, Daimler cements it — making general jurisdiction rare, rigid, and almost entirely confined to two locations.

### Identification of the Body

- **Case:** *Daimler AG v. Bauman*, 571 U.S. 117 (2014)
- **Doctrine:** General Personal Jurisdiction
- **Era:** Modern contraction
- **Reason for Autopsy:** It cements the **"at home"** rule and makes general jurisdiction exceptional.

### External Examination

The body presents with:

- Argentinian plaintiffs
- Alleged human-rights abuses in Argentina
- A German corporation (Daimler AG)
- A U.S. subsidiary (Mercedes-Benz USA)
- A lawsuit filed in California
- A central question: **Can a corporation be sued in a state simply because its subsidiary does a lot of business there?**

This is where the doctrine becomes rigid.

### Internal Examination

**Heart (Core Issue)** Is a corporation subject to general jurisdiction in a state where it engages in substantial business through a subsidiary, even if it is not incorporated or headquartered there?

**Spine (Rule of Law)** A corporation is subject to general jurisdiction only where it is **"at home."** This means:

- Place of incorporation
- Principal place of business

Only in **exceptional cases** can a corporation be "at home" elsewhere. This spine is rigid, narrow, and nearly unbreakable.

**Brain (Reasoning)** The Court reasons from predictability, fairness, and international comity:

- Daimler is a German company
- Its U.S. subsidiary's contacts cannot be automatically imputed
- Allowing general jurisdiction in California would expose Daimler to suit everywhere
- That would violate due process

The brain is focused on limiting exposure and protecting international defendants.

**Bones (General Jurisdiction Structure)** Daimler hardens the bones:

- General jurisdiction is **rare**
- "Doing business" is not enough
- Even substantial, continuous sales do not create general jurisdiction
- The corporation must be **essentially at home**

This is the skeletal frame of modern doctrine.

**Lungs (Fairness and Policy)** The doctrine breathes through:

- Predictability for corporations
- Respect for international sovereignty
- Avoiding universal jurisdiction
- Ensuring due process limits

The lungs are tight and controlled.

**Stomach (Facts Digested)** The Court digests:

- Daimler is incorporated in Germany
- Its principal place of business is in Germany
- Mercedes-Benz USA is a separate entity
- California sales, though large, are only a small slice of Daimler's global operations

These facts do not support general jurisdiction.

**Cause of Death**

Daimler kills the idea that:

- A corporation can be sued anywhere it does substantial business
- Subsidiary contacts automatically count
- General jurisdiction is broad or flexible
- "Continuous and systematic" contacts are enough

General jurisdiction becomes skeletal and rare.

**Toxicology Report**

External forces influencing the decision:

- Globalization of corporations
- Concern about forum shopping

- International diplomatic considerations
- Need for predictable rules for multinational companies
- Fear of exposing foreign corporations to worldwide litigation

The doctrine reflects a world where corporations operate globally but due process remains territorial.

### Fractures and Weak Points

Even this rigid skeleton has fractures:

- What counts as an "exceptional case"?
- How to treat temporary headquarters?
- What about companies with dispersed operations?
- How to handle digital or online presence?

These fractures remain unresolved and appear in later cases like *Ford Motor Co.*

### Surviving Relatives

Daimler strengthens:

- Goodyear's "at home" rule
- Hanson's defendant-centered analysis
- Volkswagen's foreseeability limits
- Shoe's fairness principles

It becomes the controlling rule for general jurisdiction.

### Future Prognosis

Daimler remains the modern standard:

- General jurisdiction is extremely limited
- Most cases must rely on specific jurisdiction

- Courts rarely find corporations "at home" outside their state of incorporation or headquarters
- The doctrine is stable but rigid

This is the final tightening of the bones.

**Variable Manipulation**

Changing one fact changes the outcome:

- If Daimler were incorporated in California → general jurisdiction
- If its principal place of business were in California → general jurisdiction
- If Daimler temporarily relocated its headquarters to California → possible exceptional case

This teaches students how to analyze corporate identity with precision.

**Mini Lab:**

Suppose Daimler moved its North American headquarters to California for five years while renovating its New Jersey offices. Would California be an "exceptional case" under *Daimler*?

## *Bristol-Myers Squibb Co. v. Superior Court (2017):* Full Legal Autopsy

This is the cadaver that stitches the doctrine into its modern, precise form. It limits specific jurisdiction in multi-plaintiff and mass-tort cases and clarifies that **contacts must connect to the claim, not just to the defendant**. After decades of doctrinal expansion and contraction, this case sharpens the scalpel.

### Identification of the Body

- **Case:** *Bristol-Myers Squibb Co. v. Superior Court*, 582 U.S. 255 (2017)
- **Doctrine:** Specific Personal Jurisdiction
- **Era:** Modern precision
- **Reason for Autopsy:** It tightens the "arise out of or relate to" requirement and restricts state courts from hearing claims by out-of-state plaintiffs.

### External Examination

The body presents with:

- Hundreds of plaintiffs suing over the drug Plavix
- Some plaintiffs from California
- Many plaintiffs from other states
- A defendant (BMS) with extensive business in California
- A central question: **Can California hear claims from non-California plaintiffs when the drug was not designed, manufactured, or purchased there?**

This is where the doctrine becomes surgical.

**Internal Examination**

**Heart (Core Issue)** Does specific jurisdiction exist when the defendant has extensive forum contacts, but the plaintiffs' claims do **not** arise from those contacts?

**Spine (Rule of Law)** There must be a **connection between the forum and the specific claims at issue**. This means:

- The defendant's forum contacts must cause, give rise to, or relate to the plaintiff's claim.
- General business activity in the forum is not enough.

This spine is precise and rigid.

**Brain (Reasoning)** The Court reasons from claim-specific fairness:

- BMS sold Plavix nationwide
- But the out-of-state plaintiffs did not buy, ingest, or suffer harm from Plavix in California
- California had no connection to their claims
- Allowing jurisdiction would create nationwide exposure in any state where the defendant does business

The brain is focused on limiting forum overreach.

**Muscles (Specific Jurisdiction Structure)** The doctrine flexes through:

- Defendant's contacts with the forum
- Connection between those contacts and the claim
- Claim-specific analysis
- Fairness and predictability

These muscles make the doctrine strong and controlled.

**Lungs (Tests Applied)** The doctrine breathes through:

- Purposeful availment
- Claim-connection requirement
- Fairness factors
- Federalism concerns

The lungs are tight and efficient.

**Stomach (Facts Digested)** The Court digests:

- BMS had research facilities in California
- BMS sold Plavix in California
- But the out-of-state plaintiffs:
    - did not buy Plavix in California
    - did not ingest it in California
    - were not injured in California
    - had no claim-specific connection to California

These facts do not support specific jurisdiction.

**Cause of Death**

BMS kills the idea that:

- A defendant's general business activity creates specific jurisdiction
- Mass-tort plaintiffs can sue in a single favorable state
- "Relate to" is broad
- Nationwide conduct creates nationwide jurisdiction

Specific jurisdiction becomes precise and claim-focused.

### Toxicology Report

External forces influencing the decision:

- Rise of mass-tort litigation
- Forum shopping concerns
- Federalism and state sovereignty
- Desire for predictable jurisdictional rules
- Corporate fairness considerations

The doctrine reflects a need for claim-specific limits.

### Fractures and Weak Points

Even this precise body has fractures:

- How narrow is "relate to"?
- What about nationwide marketing campaigns?
- What about digital contacts?
- How does this apply to class actions?

These fractures are partially addressed in *Ford Motor Co. v. Montana* (2021), which softens the edges.

### Surviving Relatives

BMS strengthens:

- Hanson's purposeful availment
- Volkswagen's foreseeability limits
- Burger King's relationship analysis
- Daimler's "at home" rule (by contrast)

It becomes the modern rule for specific jurisdiction.

### Future Prognosis

BMS remains essential because it:

- Limits specific jurisdiction
- Prevents forum shopping
- Requires claim-specific connections
- Shapes modern multi-plaintiff litigation
- Influences digital-contact cases

It completes the modern personal-jurisdiction body.

### Variable Manipulation

Changing one fact changes the outcome:

- If the out-of-state plaintiffs bought Plavix in California → jurisdiction
- If BMS designed or manufactured Plavix in California → stronger connection
- If the marketing campaign was California-specific → possible jurisdiction

This teaches students how to analyze claim-connection.

### Mini Lab:

Suppose BMS ran a nationwide advertising campaign from its California research facility, and the out-of-state plaintiffs saw those ads in their home states. Does this create specific jurisdiction under *Bristol-Myers Squibb*?

## *Ford Motor Co. v. Montana Eighth Judicial District Court (2021):* Full Legal Autopsy

This is the cadaver that softens the sharp edges of *Bristol-Myers Squibb* and clarifies the modern meaning of **"arise out of or relate to."** It is the case that restores flexibility without returning to chaos — the doctrine's final, living organ.

### Identification of the Body

- **Case:** *Ford Motor Co. v. Montana Eighth Judicial District Court*, 592 U.S. ___ (2021)
- **Doctrine:** Specific Personal Jurisdiction
- **Era:** Modern clarification
- **Reason for Autopsy:** It explains that a claim need not be caused by the defendant's forum contacts — it only needs to **relate to** them.

### External Examination

The body presents with:

- Two separate accidents (Montana and Minnesota)
- Ford vehicles involved in both accidents
- Ford heavily marketing, selling, and servicing the same models in those states
- Ford arguing "no jurisdiction" because *these* specific cars were not sold in those states
- A central question: **Must the defendant's forum contacts *cause* the plaintiff's injury?**

This is where the doctrine regains flexibility.

### Internal Examination

**Heart (Core Issue)** Does specific jurisdiction require strict causation, or is it enough that the defendant extensively cultivated the forum market for the very product involved?

**Spine (Rule of Law)** A claim must **arise out of OR relate to** the defendant's forum contacts. This means:

- Causation is not required
- A strong relationship between the defendant's forum activities and the product at issue is enough

This spine is flexible but structured.

**Brain (Reasoning)** The Court reasons from realistic market behavior:

- Ford extensively marketed the same models in the forum states
- Ford sold and serviced thousands of similar vehicles there
- Ford cultivated the market for the exact product line involved
- The accidents occurred in the forum states

The brain concludes: **Ford should reasonably anticipate being sued where it markets and services the very product that caused the injury.**

**Muscles (Specific Jurisdiction Structure)** The doctrine flexes through:

- Defendant's purposeful availment
- Product-line targeting
- Market cultivation
- Claim-relationship analysis

These muscles restore strength without overreach.

**Lungs (Tests Applied)** The doctrine breathes through:

- Realistic foreseeability
- Market-based connections
- Fairness to plaintiffs and defendants
- State interest in regulating local injuries

The lungs expand after BMS's tight constriction.

**Stomach (Facts Digested)** The Court digests:

- Ford sold and serviced the same model vehicles in the forum states
- Ford advertised heavily in those states
- The accidents occurred in those states
- The plaintiffs were residents of those states

These facts support jurisdiction even without strict causation.

**Cause of Death**

Ford kills the idea that:

- Specific jurisdiction requires strict causation
- A defendant can avoid jurisdiction by pointing to the car's original sale location
- BMS created a rigid, narrow rule

The doctrine becomes realistic and product-focused.

**Toxicology Report**

External forces influencing the decision:

- National product distribution
- Modern consumer mobility
- Corporate marketing strategies

- State interest in regulating local injuries
- Need for doctrinal clarity after BMS

The doctrine reflects a modern, mobile marketplace.

### Fractures and Weak Points

Even this clarified body has fractures:

- How broad is "relate to"?
- What about online sales?
- What about products with diffuse supply chains?
- How does this apply to nationwide digital platforms?

These fractures remain open for future cases.

### Surviving Relatives

Ford strengthens:

- Shoe's fairness
- Hanson's purposeful availment
- Volkswagen's foreseeability
- Burger King's relationship analysis
- BMS's claim-specific requirement (but softens it)

It becomes the modern articulation of specific jurisdiction.

### Future Prognosis

Ford remains essential because it:

- Restores flexibility to specific jurisdiction
- Clarifies "relate to"
- Prevents defendants from evading suit through technicalities

- Balances fairness with predictability

It is the doctrine's final, living organ.

**Variable Manipulation**

Changing one fact changes the outcome:

- If Ford did not market or service the model in the forum → weaker connection
- If the accident occurred in another state → weaker connection
- If the plaintiff was injured elsewhere → weaker connection

This teaches students how to analyze modern product-based jurisdiction.

**Mini Lab:**

Suppose Ford marketed the model nationwide but did not sell or service that model in the forum state. Does the claim still "relate to" Ford's forum contacts under *Ford Motor Co.*?

# Synthesis Chapter

## The Living Body of Personal Jurisdiction

Personal Jurisdiction is not a list of cases. It is a living organism — one that has grown, fractured, healed, and reshaped itself over nearly 150 years. After dissecting each case under the scalpel, this chapter steps back from the operating table to examine the doctrine as a whole body.

**This is where the pieces become a system.**

### The Evolutionary Anatomy of the Doctrine

#### 1. The Skeleton — Pennoyer v. Neff (1877)

The doctrine begins with rigid territorial bones. Power is physical. Presence is everything. The body cannot bend.

#### 2. The Heart — International Shoe (1945)

The skeleton is replaced with a beating heart of fairness and minimum contacts. The doctrine becomes alive, flexible, and functional.

#### 3. The First Breath — McGee (1957)

A single purposeful contact can sustain jurisdiction. The lungs expand.

#### 4. The Backbone — Hanson (1958)

Purposeful availment becomes the spine. Without it, the doctrine collapses into limitless reach.

#### 5. The Brain — World-Wide Volkswagen (1980)

The doctrine learns to think. Foreseeability of product travel ≠ foreseeability of being sued.

#### 6. The Muscles — Burger King (1985)

Contracts create deliberate affiliation. The doctrine gains strength, nuance, and movement.

### 7. The Fractured Skull — Asahi (1987)

Two competing brains emerge. Stream of commerce splits into two incompatible theories. The doctrine suffers a traumatic injury that never fully heals.

### 8. The Narrowing Bones — Goodyear (2011)

General jurisdiction shrinks. "Continuous and systematic" is no longer enough.

### 9. The Rigid Skeleton — Daimler (2014)

General jurisdiction becomes nearly immovable. "At home" means two places — and almost never anywhere else.

### 10. The Surgical Precision — Bristol-Myers Squibb (2017)

Specific jurisdiction becomes claim-specific. Contacts must connect to *this* plaintiff's claim.

### 11. The Modern Organism — Ford Motor Co. (2021)

"Relate to" regains flexibility. Causation is not required. Realistic market behavior matters.

## The Modern Body: How Personal Jurisdiction Works Today

### General Jurisdiction (The Bones)

A corporation is "at home" in:

- its place of incorporation
- its principal place of business

Only in *exceptional* cases can it be "at home" elsewhere.

This is a rigid skeleton.

### Specific Jurisdiction (The Organs)

Specific jurisdiction requires:

- purposeful availment (the spine)
- minimum contacts (the heart)
- fairness (the lungs)
- a claim that arises out of or relates to those contacts (the brain)

This is the living, breathing part of the doctrine.

## Exam-Ready Flowcharts

*Civil Procedure: Personal Jurisdiction — Law Under the Scalpel: Case Dissections*

*Law in Pieces Series*

## Flowchart 1 — The Personal Jurisdiction Master Algorithm

### Step 1 — Identify the Type of Jurisdiction

- Is the plaintiff asking for **general jurisdiction**?
- Or **specific jurisdiction**?

If unclear → analyze **both.**

### Flowchart 2 — General Jurisdiction ("At Home")

**1. Is the defendant an individual?**

- **Yes** → Are they **domiciled** in the forum?
  - If yes → **General jurisdiction exists.**
  - If no → **General jurisdiction fails.**

**2. Is the defendant a corporation?**

Ask two questions:

- **Place of incorporation?**
  - If the forum is the state of incorporation → **General jurisdiction exists.**
- **Principal place of business?**
  - If the forum is the nerve center → **General jurisdiction exists.**

**3. If neither applies → Is this an "exceptional case"?**

- Does the corporation have operations so substantial that it is **essentially at home** in the forum?
- *Daimler* says this is **rare**.

If no → **General jurisdiction fails.**

## Flowchart 3 — Specific Jurisdiction (Three-Part Test)

Specific jurisdiction requires **all three**:

### Part 1 — Purposeful Availment (The Spine)

Did the defendant **deliberately reach into the forum**?

Ask:

- Did they advertise, sell, negotiate, contract, or target the forum?
- Did they cultivate the market?
- Did they supervise or direct activities into the forum?
- Or are the contacts **unilateral**, **accidental**, or **consumer-created**?

If no purposeful availment → **Specific jurisdiction fails.**

### Part 2 — Connection Between Contacts and Claim (The Brain)

**A. Does the claim "arise out of" the contacts?**

- Direct causation → Yes.

**B. Does the claim "relate to" the contacts?**

- Product-line targeting (*Ford*) → Yes.
- General business activity with no link (*BMS*) → No.

If no connection → **Specific jurisdiction fails.**

### Part 3 — Fairness (The Lungs)

Even with contacts, jurisdiction must be **fair**.

Consider:

- Burden on defendant
- Forum state's interest
- Plaintiff's interest in convenient relief
- Judicial efficiency
- Shared policy interests

If unfair → **Specific jurisdiction fails.**

If fair → **Specific jurisdiction exists.**

## Flowchart 4 — Stream of Commerce (Asahi Split)

Use this flowchart **only** when the defendant is a component manufacturer or part of a distribution chain.

### Step 1 — Did the defendant place the product into the stream of commerce?

If no → Stream of commerce analysis ends.

If yes → Move to the split.

### Step 2 — Apply BOTH Tests (No Majority Rule)

### A. O'Connor's Stream of Commerce PLUS

Requires:

- Advertising in the forum
- Designing the product for the forum
- Customer service channels in the forum
- Distributor targeting the forum

If no PLUS → No purposeful availment.

### B. Brennan's Pure Stream of Commerce

Requires:

- Awareness that the product will reach the forum
- Regular, predictable flow of goods

If awareness exists → Purposeful availment satisfied.

### Step 3 — Fairness (All Justices Agree)

Even if contacts exist, ask:

- Is jurisdiction fair?
- Is the burden severe?
- Is the forum's interest minimal?
- Are international concerns present?

If unfair → **No jurisdiction.**

## Flowchart 5 — The PJ Exam Answer Template

This is the structure students should follow on every exam.

### 1. Start with General Jurisdiction

- Is the defendant "at home"?
- If not → move on.

### 2. Purposeful Availment

- Identify the defendant's deliberate contacts.
- Distinguish unilateral actions.
- Use *Hanson*, *Volkswagen*, *Burger King*, *Ford*.

### 3. Connection Between Contacts and Claim

- Apply *BMS* (narrow).
- Apply *Ford* (flexible).
- Explain whether the claim arises out of or relates to the contacts.

**4. Fairness**

- Apply the fairness factors.
- Use *Asahi* for burden analysis.
- Use *Shoe* for overall fairness.

**5. Conclude Clearly**

- State whether jurisdiction exists.
- Tie back to the strongest facts.

## Flowchart 6 — Quick-Reference Case Map

A one-glance summary of which case governs which issue.

- **Territorial Power** → *Pennoyer*
- **Minimum Contacts** → *International Shoe*
- **Single Contact Rule** → *McGee*
- **Purposeful Availment** → *Hanson*
- **Foreseeability Limits** → *Volkswagen*
- **Contracts & Relationships** → *Burger King*
- **Stream of Commerce Split** → *Asahi*
- **General Jurisdiction Narrowed** → *Goodyear*
- **General Jurisdiction Rigid** → *Daimler*
- **Claim-Specific Connection** → *BMS*
- **“Relates To” Clarified** → *Ford*

## Glossary of Anatomical Terms

## *Law Under the Scalpel: Case Dissections — Law in Pieces Series*

This glossary defines the anatomical metaphors used throughout the *Law Under the Scalpel* series. Each term corresponds to a doctrinal function, helping students visualize how a case "lives," "moves," and "evolves" within the body of the law.

### Heart — The Core Issue

The central question the court must resolve. The heart pumps life into the case: without understanding the issue, the rest of the doctrine cannot function.

### Spine — The Rule of Law

The structural rule that supports the doctrine. The spine holds the case upright and connects it to the broader legal framework. A weak spine means a fragile doctrine.

### Brain — The Court's Reasoning

The intellectual engine of the case. The brain explains *why* the court reached its conclusion and reveals the logic, policy, and analytical pathways that shape the doctrine.

### Lungs — The Tests and Standards

The doctrinal tests that allow the rule to "breathe" in real cases. These include multi-factor tests, fairness analyses, foreseeability standards, and balancing frameworks.

### Stomach — The Facts Digested

The essential facts that the court metabolizes into its holding. These are the facts that matter — the ones that feed the rule and shape the outcome.

**Bones — The Structural Framework**

The foundational elements of the doctrine that remain stable over time. Bones represent the durable, long-term architecture of the legal body.

**Muscles — The Moving Parts**

The flexible, functional components that allow the doctrine to adapt. Muscles represent multi-factor tests, relationship analyses, and practical considerations.

**Skin — The Surface-Level Holding**

The outward result of the case — what the court ultimately decided. Skin is visible, but it does not reveal the deeper anatomy beneath.

**Fractures — Weaknesses and Unresolved Tensions**

Points where the doctrine cracks. These include concurrences, splits, ambiguities, and doctrinal conflicts that create future litigation.

**Toxicology Report — External Influences**

Historical, economic, political, or social forces that shaped the court's decision. These reveal the environment in which the doctrine evolved.

**Cause of Death — What the Case Overrules or Replaces**

The doctrinal ideas, tests, or assumptions that the case kills or transforms. This shows how the law evolves through autopsy.

**Future Prognosis — The Case's Legacy**

How the case influences later doctrine. Prognosis predicts the case's long-term health, impact, and role in the legal body.

**Variable Manipulation — Fact Pattern Sensitivity**

How small factual changes alter the outcome. This teaches students to think like lawyers by testing the doctrine's limits.

### Mini Lab — Student Application Exercise

A short, targeted hypothetical that allows the reader to apply the case's anatomy to a new scenario. This reinforces mastery through practice.

## Closing Note

Thank you for walking through this body with me.

Personal Jurisdiction can be a challenging doctrines in Civil Procedure, not because it is impossible, but because we learn differently, there is not a one size fits all approach to learning. My hope is that this volume has given you not only understanding, but confidence — the sense that the doctrine is no longer a maze, but a map.

You now know its heart, its spine, its fractures, and its evolution. You can see how each case fits into the living organism of the law. And most importantly, you can carry this clarity into exams, practice, and the next stages of your legal education.

In the next volume, we turn to **Subject Matter Jurisdiction** — the second great gateway of Civil Procedure, and another doctrine that becomes far easier once its anatomy is revealed.

Until then, keep your scalpel sharp.

— **Anjanette G. Seymour**

# ABOUT THE AUTHOR

**Anjanette G. Seymour** is a visionary legal educator, compliance professional, and author dedicated to transforming the way students learn law. With a background spanning legal research, compliance, governance, and narrative-driven pedagogy, she brings a unique blend of clarity, creativity, and emotional intelligence to every project. She is the creator of the **Law in Pieces** brand — a learning philosophy that blends storytelling, doctrine, and visual memory tools to give students the "aha" moments they deserve. Her work bridges the gap between dense legal theory and real human understanding.

Anjanette G. Seymour holds an LL.M., an LL.B. (Hons.), and a Bachelor of Science in Business Administration, along with certification as a Risk & Compliance Management Professional (CRCMP). She has authored numerous books, study guides, and bilingual legal resources designed to empower learners across backgrounds.
Her mission is simple: **Make law accessible. Make law human. Make law unforgettable.**

You can explore more of her work at: **anjanettegseymour.com**

www.ingramcontent.com/pod-product-compliance
Lightning Source LLC
LaVergne TN
LVHW022022200926
848481LV00007B/2494
*9798995892366*